For Liorah and her wonderful Daddy.
We love and miss you Mike. – CF

With love to all my family in Australia. – BC

SIMON & SCHUSTER

Celebrating 100 Years of Publishing Since 1924
First published in Great Britain in 2024 by Simon & Schuster UK Ltd
1st Floor, 222 Gray's Inn Road, London WC1X 8HB

A CIP catalogue record for this book is available from
the British Library upon request

ISBN: 978-1-4711-6590-0 (HB)
ISBN: 978-1-4711-6591-7 (PB)
ISBN: 978-1-4711-6592-4 (eBook)

Printed in China

1 3 5 7 9 10 8 6 4 2

DRAGONS LOVE
UNDERPANTS

CLAIRE FREEDMAN & BEN CORT

SIMON & SCHUSTER
London New York Sydney Toronto New Delhi

Huge scaly DRAGONS roamed the land
In long gone Days of Olde.
They LOVED to wear big underpants
In colours bright and bold.

But the dragons had a problem, BAH!
Their new pants didn't last.
They accidentally scorched them all,
Those underpants burnt fast!

There was ONE place they'd find more pants –
The Kingdom of Pantasia!
Ruled by pants-mad King Top-Bot,
Nowhere could be pants crazier!

"Let's fly there now," the dragons roared,
"And frighten Top-Bot silly!
We'll scare the pants off EVERYONE
And nose-dive Princess Tilly!"

"Help, DRAGONS!" cried the villagers.
They all fled in despair,
"Not only do they shoot out flames –
They steal our underwear!"

The king sent out his loyal knight
To fight the dragons back.
But poor Sir Y-Front legged it from
The dragon-sized attack!

The dragons snatched King Top-Bot. Gasp!

And flew away – alack!

"The scoundrels!" Princess Tilly cried,

"How will we get him back?"

The palace got a ransom note . . .
"We've got King Top-Bot here!
If you don't send us piles of pants,
We'll scorch him on the rear!"

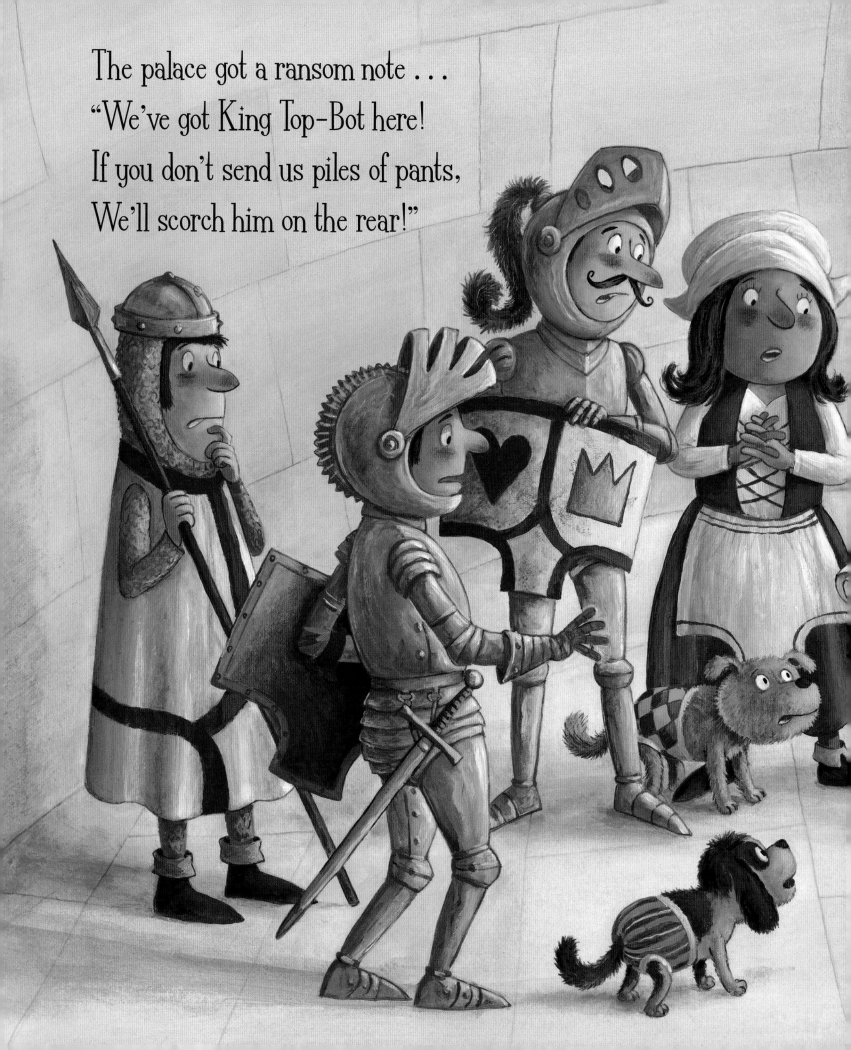

"Don't panic!" Princess Tilly said,
"I've got a plan. It's clever!
We'll get King Top-Bot safely home
And stop those beasts forever!"

Quick! Tilly hurried to the forge,
What was she going to do?
CLINK CLANK BANG! She set to work,
All night her hammer flew!

At daybreak, with Sir Y-Front's help
She loaded up a wagon,
"GO! GIDDY-UP!" they urged the horse,
"It's time to meet a DRAGON!"

SURPRISE! They brought them METAL pants!
The dragons cheered with glee,
"These pants will last FOREVER!"
And they set King Top-Bot free!

The king threw a huge party.
There was dancing, fun and laughter,
And everyone – the dragons too –
Lived happily ever after!

So be glad you're not a dragon,
Wearing underpants that creak,
Or all your friends would laugh and joke,
"Who made that AWFUL squeak?"